MILK FEVER

MILK FEVER

POEMS BY

MEGAN ROSS

UHLANGA

2018

Published in Cape Town, South Africa by uHlanga in 2018

UHLANGAPRESS.CO.ZA

Distributed outside South Africa by the African Books Collective

AFRICANBOOKSCOLLECTIVE.COM

ISBN: 978-0-620-79227-1

Edited by Nick Mulgrew

Cover art by Leora Joy
Cover design by Nick Mulgrew

Proofread by Maya Surya Pillay

The body text of this book is set in Garamond Premier Pro 11PT on 15PT

☙

Versions of some of the poems in this collection were first published in the
following publications: 'Language' in *Aerodrome*, 'Nobody but my own' in *Praxis
Magazine,* 'Fishing for sharks at midnight' in *New Contrast*, 'Catching the sun'
in *New Coin*, 'untitled' in *The Kalahari Review*. Previous versions of 'Love in the
year of bleeding' and 'Silence is the rain falling silence is the hand around your neck'
were longlisted for the 2017 EU Sol Plaatje European Union Award and
were published in that competition's anthology.

To Oliver Micah,
my light. Without you,
there would be no poetry.

CONTENTS

"Every story I have ever told has a kind of breach to it, I think. You could say that my writing isn't quite right. That all the beginnings have endings in them."
    – LIDIA YUKNAVITCH, 'WOVEN'

"Silence taunts: a dare. Everything that disappears Disappears as if returning somewhere."
    – TRACY K. SMITH, 'THE UNIVERSE: ORIGINAL MOTION PICTURE SOUNDTRACK'

Object

Love is a mou   outh & Mother is no verb.
She is space & time crystallised in noun, festooned across a hospital ward,
its solar system trembling with the world's end, elastic tongues wrapped
around the flattened globe.

At night when it is the city's turn to light the sky,
she dreams of creation splitting open under teacher's pen,
ink-spliced parts dictated by biology, geography, mathematics, cosmology.
(as if time really is an endpoint a corporeal destination as if seas really do part)

Could I embody this noun, anagram I?   Spit consonant
as easily as my name. Proper noun, a knot swished
around the infested mouth of this town. Resist synecdoche.
Verbs roost in the attic, clipping their own wings in beak-nips because
they cannot do what they are meant to do, won't do, but suppose to.

Soft grey feathers lose colour to the sky.

Do you suppose that one day I might transpose melody upon even the dullest swathe of sentence,
    Trojan language with our amaranth & cochineal insides
locker-hidden & quiet   spray the town milky gold,
    rest my swollen breasts
like two loaded pistols on the back of the lady in front of us,
    who startles when she reads the map of veins across my chest & knows where love grows,
knows my trigger.

Might we club the sentence till it splits open starfruit cracked & bleeding now oozing dying now
    giving life now
disgusting & startling as durian struck & halved in the iced cart of a Bangkok fruit man
    opening spaghetti-guts tin-can garish in the cold clean of the oт

I know what   I do   I do   , we'll send a signal

to our sisters   *yes,*   *I do,*

something other than metaphor

the word itself   we'll push it downstream

& paint our doors with our own blood:

roaring   *even without sons we still*

are & our bodies want no syntax we slip

into the river unbidden each sentence of skin

your last lust's final fear   punctuate us

if you dare

Armageddon Summer

I sewed your name into my
      heel. I was 15 & a
fool. I let it swim under
      my skin & breathe smoke into
my veins, confusing the heat
      with something living, not a
dead star orbiting wet ga
      laxies. I didn't know then
that we were rivers: that we
      would trace our blood to the same
source & swim south toward the

ocean, that you would ragged
      tooth this world from my body
& spit helium into
      my blood-wetted lungs. Did I
somehow mistake your fist for
      love, & eel it inside my
mouth, press my anemone
      tongue to your heliotrope
teeth? Or did we simply burn
      our December skins, reli
shing their Coca-Cola blanch

   & shining pink. Small eyes blink
ing for the first time inside.
    Each brand new cut: our begging
for voice; the fetid blisters
    cursed to scales, our slashed wrists re
sisting the gills we longed for.
    Tempting as vodka, broken
as glass, we lost our legs to
    tails; wrote our names in next-day
vomit. Lone holography.

That was the summer we closed
    around each other like stone
walls, thinking love immortal,
    as if we were speaking the
language of our futures &
    not the ancient light of stars.
We didn't know that in this
    drowning world our skins are salt
& desert is the song of
    girls unborn, who soon dream of
their own small deaths. We thought mood
    rings fair trade for mulberries;
laddered arms friendship's true price.

    We split our lot with fish &
left our bodies to the sun.

Nothing in the water

1

your milk comes apart   so it can   be held
like soft frangipanis   inking   your skin

poison in them   somewhere   mother's old
reminder   in your cheeks   under
your tongue   over your eyes   two
coins   the price of
seasons   wet between your legs

/

steam-train   kisses   led   us here
to your tightened middle   to every Googled image
of
our December   revolt against   the heavens
each swallowed promise   of hell   lining

your stomach   you've known the miracles:
spinal fluid &   sonar   port stains
hitching lifts on Cupid's bow   / genes
riding shotgun   on chance   then
after
milk-sticky   & stapled   all
crepe paper   & pearlescent
                 stitches hurting

/

we both wonder: would I have taken
                         your boombox shape
                         your transistor hiss   that static
                         beneath   your breath?
there was some   idea of   me lost
between your teeth

/

you lay down a woman   & stand up a ghost
not having died   but mouthing it
counting   the lumps   like soured   milk
your friend   once drank   on her period   &
then your   thighs are unsticking   in the
place   we say goodbye
          & where we last lay   together
silhouettes   stain   the grass   piss yellow
as if   someone   slept on that
lawn   for a month (more)   as if   her bones
were leeched of
light   as all of   the planes   in her
thirst for   rain
I never return.

Another bird pirouettes across the telephone line,
romancing electricity with her feathers
& her blood. This sticky Rembrandt:
look how she toys with the sun.
Somehow death feels closer today. How
difficult it is to love like this, knowing loss
is always near; knowing that sometimes,
you are the loss.

refrigerator eggs stained to   teeth & bone

there's blood in the yellow   small bodies

like Maraschino cherries   topping trifle
at Christmas   seams   of custard like sallow
thighs   of a newish corpse
wobbling cellulite-y on my spoon   I wonder
how different are they from a slide of brain?

what secrets lie at their meet?
each swollen hemisphere is   like some
sugar-coated slice   of *it's-the-holidays-why*
-are-you-so-glum?   all your still born-dreams
in neon jelly that's   nothing like   lime

/

If you must know   I ate them   anyway
          ~~knowing death whenever I seek it~~

          humming   *one day I will crack open*
                              and know my yolk

Origin myths

I should have guessed I would always take to mourning like religion.
I swallowed the loss of my mother's father inside her womb,
death sampling my blood /
lumped with absence. My futures bloomed in some prior-ticking heart

& I forget this (when it's my turn to swallow the world.)
I think it should show in some mark, believing myself
hemisphered & tectonic, wanting the bliss of tides,
not his emerald eyes, craving love but not the sapphire of morning song

while in a ruby-winged autumn, under my skin, a butterfly changes shape.
Why do I contemplate my life as if all my mothers
never sewed dreams into my eyes, as if all my time
isn't a blade bleeding someone else's thigh?

/

I've spent too much time in parking lots   I think
tasting tar   all I shouldn't   *my nails are never clean*
who I would have been if I had Instagram at 13?   I miss
videos   &   Presticking posters to my wall   surf wax sticking
to my   garden path   wishing my breasts were bigger.

The tooth fairy took my teeth but my mother hid
my molars   with her pearls   threading
my pupil through   her mother's iris
whose death   planted Sahara
between   her daughter & granddaughter.   how to flood a
desert?   You can't   which is the curse of alleles

& the sum   of loss   grief's sweet weight
a haunting we shall go, a haunting   we shall go

in this shop of horrors: where daughters know
their   mother's mother   only in photos
only in second-hand memories   knowing she would have
loved you   only by the
echoes   in your mother
how lonely
                is this:

calling someone a name when she is a stranger
when she does not know mine
when her daughter clasps her compact longing to touch

the face locked inside glass

her scent less potent
each time it opens

/

like a mother a writer must have knowledge of necromancy
she must be crowned clairvoyant

/

In the old back room that my parents fixed for me, the one with the naked bulb I thought romantic, where the paint chipped like old nail varnish & the roving damp was hair set alight I watched my legs disappear as if they were twin Disprins dropped into the fizz of a glass. I'd lost my toes in Bangkok, on a winter's day in mismatched pumps, the air so thick it hurt to breathe, & then my feet snapped apart in stirrups, moon-faced gynae & her no options (but to keep the baby

   the baby. it's just a   –.) My ankles went then, next my nerves, on a plane between here *& the* DMC *will cost you 20 000 Baht*, maybe after *I don't want to do this*. By July my thighs were a soggy streak, my torso an aeroplane weaving chemtrails, as if all that mattered was the abattoir blade of my middle carving clean the meat off my bones.

A premonition of a past we haven't written yet

i.

We spit our contempt into the copper pipes &
feed each length into the grass, until their

damp warmth wilts with sound, soft
trombone leaking. Each note: tea leaves

coiled to night adder, hissing & kissing.
Chalked in high accent. Sprinkled with attic

salt. From their mouths a small library
blooms, an encyclopaedia of stems & ears.

No blueprint. A dead architect. Only blush,
no bride. We lick our forefinger & thumb,

page our precedents: drunkards & nobles,
singers & queers. Our forebears keyed

cars & siphoned colour. Sugared engines.
Smashed windscreens. Practised black magic

in orphanages & inked saints into tanned
arms. Fed homes eucalyptus & beer. Built

cities from copper buckets. Warmed milk on
angry stoves. Measured time. Plotted stars.

Served pale queens on wicked thrones. Lit the
first candles in the first synagogue of this land.

Killed lovers. Faced the noose. Survived. Died.
As did everyone, really. How then does anyone

stand this template? You & I, we have no peace:
you fight until your lips blister. I have thrown more

vases than I can count. & I wish I was being
hypothetical: you almost left how many times?

We've got no damn mettle for mould. No stomach
for imitation. Not in these skins. We bruise too

easily, the evidence stays. I for one would hear the
spiders before their webs crackled with stars. You'd

split mercury. Attics are merely pretty prisons. Glass
can look like bars. & milk blackens in burning

chests. My nightmares always wallpaper themselves
in floral frieze. Right, then it's decided: I set the nursery

alight. Sell my rhinestone icons. Consecrate our new
gods in words like Saturn & Lust. When our thieving

neighbour receives incorrect accounts of a shotgun
wedding, I show the empty barrel. No diamond lust here,

I tell her. I marry for money. That's why I haven't. At the locked gates, I seize. A restless post box gapes for news.

I can't reach its mouth to pull out its tongue.

ii.
Our building chant rises like steam.
We bathe in the heat it brings,
remembering the sting.

iii.

In light soft as smoke,
        light gentle as fronds unfurling;
damp to the touch like the unknown curve of cheek
& the sweet, unmeasured weight of new flesh,
we glide through the rooms –
ghosts,
premonitions of a past we haven't written yet,
licking the plaster set soft & sticky,
sweet pudding in the crease of your spine.

In our mother-of-pearl kitchen is a sink   bristling
at the silverware;   a drawer of   tines & blades ancient
as rings,   cups & saucers: a history of lovers
awaiting fire.

iv.

He orbits the bathtub, our son of suns

– still ringless

round & slick as the roof of our mouths,
this star cut from our marbled gums,
a drink of caudle & rhyme.

v.
Rumours raised us, hearsay our parent lyric,
& naturally we understand the caveat: that *ghosts &*
                                          premonitions
                                          will enter our
                                          present,
                                                    bending time,
                                                    shifting tenses.

& by midday the floorboards hum
notes polished into oak & lime,
a tooth-&-bone hymnbook
written across time.

& the builders tut-tut here, murmuring from the pavement,
searching for the lolling concrete tongue, for facts to cure
& seize in their spluttering of machine
& we give no breath to their leave or need for certainty.

vi.

Sun turns heavy into the sea,
& tired, but not beat, we fold into brick & rust
& at dusk
we pull the ceiling taut over a ribcage of beams,
eyelid closing softly into eternal dry-wood sleep.

Semblance

I dreamt
a poem I'd never
written,
its words
the closest I'd come
to you.

untitled

You are a closed fist.
There is no knowing
what lines run
the length of
your palm,
or when it is
you will
strike.

The Book of Her

who was your human sacrifice &
did you name her before you sent her to your gods?

Irony is your father planting seeds
beneath your skin & wondering why
you bloom at a bad man's touch.

Wondering how you always find
yourself in some other volcanic mouth,
why you always end up drinking ash
when you were promised flame.

you peel back the garage door
like a skin
feeling for   the give   the lift
& wonder if each spanner nail hammer
is a part of him feeling the cool weight of each in
your palm
the Egyptian surgeon knowing the body
inside   the value of brain   the heft of heart

II(A)

a beloved's room is an exploded view

I crumple / you yell   at Black Rock
                              & my body
                              is a paper boat
skimming gutters   a stone you've
                              skipped across the ribbon of streets

it's crazy but as I run across town all I think is *get to the tennis courts* as if
sport could save me as if the sky is a motherly eye watching the hot night
snake his tendrils around my ankles, the banana moon wedged between
my toes like the gospel

I stay at a friend for two nights & can't help wonder if this is an
outcome of mottled screens /
your secret collage of dreams

who do you wish I was   when this happens?
your mother   her mother before they left
or   the mother before them –
her child a fish swimming through
his mother's mouth to the dark he thinks
he'll know   home

/

I'll give you something to cry about.

/

I'm just a sea spitting up angry men onto frightened shores,
their clenched fists of teeth & their unceasing store
of minutes furious as guns / resolute as nails
each molten hand clutching ponytails.

IV *(& STILL)*

I look for the child you were,
shooting his play-play pistols;
how he dreamt of battlefields,
how you settled for daughters.

A man's love is a naked flame

You cracked
my
spine
as you might
a book
you said you loved,
a text
you knew
by heart,
a song
you liked
to
sing.

Fishing for sharks at midnight

In your life there were three houses which counted among the ones you
    called home.
We named them for their proximity to the ocean, & their naming took
    on shapes
that peopled our memories – river house, middle house, third house.

In its monastery white & reed-lined basement of dreams,
the river house was consigned for prayer (ascetic grove),
place of rope swing & powdered tiles, shared beds below a
trap door leading to the night.

        [temple
                of wine
       history
                of spirits
       shed
                of secrets]

I only saw you there once: playing *Silent Alarm* & drinking whiskey
till midnight. He had left by then but I'd heard stories of your mother
smashing plates on the patio. Dreaming of it I am again ankle-deep
in the lagoon; I watch you fishing for sharks at midnight.

At the second house, I unfolded into scored lines & seams
while my parents rapped on the door. There we lost our hookah pipes
to an old man lus for his fix, us 13 kids curled up like kittens in the lounge.

The third house is where I joined you in that bed the weight of Mars,
bullets soaring through the yard, your cricket bat in the corner.
I think she watched us through the glass; that woman only Ma & me saw,
her hair both black & white. Sometimes I drive past 14th Ave

& remember you touching my breasts for the first time. It feels
like only yesterday we learned to reverse park in that yard.
Sometimes when I'm close I can still see you drinking whiskey in the
    garden

the story of your life taking its first breath beneath your skin.

Language

Our bodies
talk
all the
time

It's okay
I love you
Please don't

Breaking waters

Prelude:

> *they held me down, quick-quick, not a*
> *thought to my dignity*

me too friend me too

> *it's institutional violence you know*
> *they didn't even ask if I wanted an epidural*

me too friend me too

> *it's torture you know it's crazy what they do*
> *we are not animals you know*

I know friend I know

> *he made me tight as a virgin, after, friend*
> *but it hurts so much*

I know friend I know

> *sex, it hurts so much*

/

A (Water)
the knitting needle hook &
her hands that's what I remember
before the blind mouth inside me bit
a hole out of the night / a knitting needle
hook & goddamn agony

we burned a lilac-scented candle
while he waved the fan from the Chinese shop
she likened birth to a marathon in a desert:

now would you say no to water if it were offered to you?
thought so   pethodine   gas   epidural
struck off the list

& all night I swim to this mirage
& it shimmers away
& the clock has melted / natural order thwarted
& death moves through me opening me like a mouth
ventriloquist hand letting ghosts out
hold her legs open   keep her still
I am a farm animal fighting against my own meat
hold still   as if stillness can be held

& the midwife then unhitches
oceans from the sky
& I am the blood
of my first blood's promise

/

B (Bucket)
I remember when skirt-fronts were baskets for mulberries,
buckets were rock pools for crab's lone pincer, tangerine anemone –
& I want to double-knot this memory
like my daddy did my takkies

when I was four to the school photo; when being a girl was still a
liquid thing & being a mom was this play-play house-house school-
school game I put down & picked up & tried on like new shoes &
chased away with Plan B

/

C (Tear)

The outline fills
with blue / two
people stapled together
one person sewn closed

I didn't begin my life
so scarred   I grew into
the sawdust doll
by a slow succession
of seams

A life by numbers

1. at six weeks / remembering Chiang Mai / the freedom of a pool / two weeks of sun   2. & kissing in songthaews /
I sob into my own skin / contemplating shark fin soup   3. & suicide   4. I remember my options / I'm well-versed
5. as a feminist / in scripts like these / I take the number of the illegal abortionist / whose voice is a balloon whose
hands hold   6. my other future / I clutch my rent money &   7. passport / then at ten weeks the baby loosens /
I pin a bouquet of Hail Marys to my mouth / prayer blooming on my tongue   8. texting Meg Dominion: *come
quick* / palms pressed into my abdomen / sweet palm / Jerusalem / summoning futures to my fingertips / crying
baby   9. *don't leave me baby* / 31 storeys into   10. the sky & I'm mourning / someone I haven't lost yet   11. in
the ER the Thai doctor on casualty duty scans my records a field /   12. plucks anxiety a plum / bites into it / my
mind   13. a carousel / the old juice still as sweet when he calls me hysterical / just as Harry Styles belts out the
first notes of a One Direction song & the doctor answers his phone / deciding in a second breath / cervix is *OKAY /
your mind   14. not-OKAY*   15. weeks in & I'm packing tea & silk for a new life / posting boxes / boarding planes
/ in Nairobi / praying: *Jesus remember me* / land in the city of my birth   16. Johannesburg / home of mine dumps
& gold / the streets I learned to ride a bike / the home I met my mother /   17. my roots / comforting myself with
the fact that   18. in 1988 my mother made me in this same city / that she is still helping me now / even as I fear a
19. miscarriage.   20. 3 months / gynae tells me: *we don't do*   21. *abortions 'oere* & best friends sew their pleas

to my heels: *will you marry*   22. *him?* / when really what they mean is *your child is a bastard.* 7 months & my grandfather leaves to where my baby came from / home with our beginnings / returning twice to say / first: your sister, Wild Thing /   23. / sweet evidence: [Rape Survivor T] call my   24. mother; watch a family crumble & then: *it burns, Wild Thing, it burns* / & I know it's only getting   25. worse / 8 months & he's disappeared again / sunk back into his eyes / & there's no stealing him back / no finding the money to birth / it isn't free to   26. labour   27. midwife palpates & clears me for the water / at 42 weeks threats of induction / increase / push for Jesus but   28. pray for death / cut open anyway / birth a pugilist / *Go tell your aunty he's 4.36kg / Jussie but*   29. *you're so small?* / 3 months in /   30. I kiss my forehead to the / kitchen floor   31. next day I'm clutching diagnosis   32. & espiride & water weight   33. six months / I look at him   34. don't trust myself   35. to be his mom / dream his little face underwater /   36. dream I follow him under   37. 10 months his daddy's sick / stumbling around a doctor's note   38. taking care of the bleeding   39. 17 months / two years since   40. the beginning & I'm swallowing   41. four pills / belly contorting   42. knowing it's right   43. knowing pain will never leave   44. & then my home is gone / people playing games / standard fuckery / draw your own conclusions / this shit goes on / & on & if you paint it / by numbers / you'll soon find   45. a picture where / your life once was

Anaphora

the veil
　　lifts
& for a moment
　　　there is no death
　　　　but time

Birth rite

Theatre (of war)
final curtain call; incision.
Perform. In the wings:
snow-capped angels of
mercy, clasping 10-blade
prayers.

Baby Is Transverse
       and I am a
an abacus of bone
       spine /
numerical
       fist of vertebrae
throating needle, a
       methylated dream
doused in oxytocin
       set alight:

theatre of
       spores
allegra of doctors
       arabesque arms many hands
a pause
       then
curtain call
       surgical waterfall
becoming deuteragonist.

Nothing is round as
     swimming pools
or beach balls with
     lost
segments longing
     for crayon or CDs
falling from
     rear-view mirrors
and R5s jingling in
     the torn lining of
a primary school blazer.

     Tripwire thighs
return to old fault lines
     garden path apocalypse
caved rooms of green
     dark as comet areolas
the clean knife of sunrise
     the wet emptying of birth
the smoke of new sound.

This bed a loom
        my limbs unspooling
insipid tapestry
        with feathered ends
a pethodine smile
        splits my face
on aberrant lines.

A radio spits into
        the room
two curses /
        no nurses /
the 7 a.m. news
        (a forecast of rain).

Mourning song

– five days in, September 29

A. I Just Died At Birth
Corpse is the first word I write after giving birth.
They call this baby blues, but I spit it, a curse
& set the mould for a motherhood I never
asked for.

/

B. Drowning
Ignorance
is a rain
that drenches,

the baby
both lifeboat
& wave.

/

C. Sarcophagus
Skin can accommodate absence,
but the womb mourns her loss,

marking each hour without
your metronome of kicks.

/

D. How do I mourn myself?
In a bathroom I wash without the light
cannot bear the hanging jacket of flesh /
this unborn death hollows me like a gem squash:
dark's green shell, sunlight's yellow seeds
somewhere else / now.

Silence is the rain falling silence is the hand around your neck

Out at Sunrise-on-sea, at Julie's house, Gabby's mom, we're house sitting
for the weekend, a clever thought were we actually well, but we're not.
A hum in the air, the bush whispering, a murmur really, should have listened,
no leaves are really that green, God was trying to tell us something which he
does. He does. Your body did in any case / remember? You couldn't pick
Oli up. It was as if you were in a vice / as if a row of teeth had settled around
your intestines. / Little bites. / I still joked that nothing could be as bad as being
bit while you're breastfeeding / that nothing was as awful as bloody milk.

We didn't know. We watched Leo bury himself in a bear carcass & I
could feel that same hole blistering in on itself, eye inside blinking furious.
Dilating with the dark / what a lark / I always had a knack for haunting
& the night swims through me, clean as a knife pulled from my
stomach, drawing blood & sound to the knot of bone grown stiff around my
heart / & I ignored you thinking you dramatic / heeding instead the images
I dreamt through Oli's cries / a neck distorting in a mouth of rope /

a body dangling from the beams / the beams / where are the beams & I'm off searching, log in my eye, hope in my throat, convinced that what lies outside of me is far worse than what now breathes in me / as if houses never swallowed misery. /

I'm wrong.

Even as I drag the camp cot out of the room / his cry its own soft storm / even as I ignore the strange clicking inside my head / night's drone / I am convinced that what lies outside of me is worse than what lives in me. / That's denial right? That's some square poltergeist shit / that's that Mifoprostol kick / that Sertraline kiss / that's what they mean when they say / going postal / postal as if you're only words on a page / as if you were ever anything / more & I think what made it worse / is by definition I was near / psychotic / that by the time you woke I already lived two nights / a year inside your sleep / latching our baby to my breast / knowing I woke his hunger for poison / a thirst we'll know in time / & do all mothers chew their discontent / while holding misery between their teeth / do all the things we leave unsaid / grow wings &

fling their meaning away to distant lands / where under the earth / soft creatures scurry about lining their nests / with secrets. Maybe in some other place / another time / I am harboured & held by older mothers / who wear their truth / like armour / who aren't any less mothers for being honest / who offer to hold my baby / so I can sleep. For who really loves a body / quietened to ash / a skin that is a burial ground / or a tongue that can not / will not / could not / would not / should not / speak?

Women with houses for heads

– after Louise Bourgeois

I pretend I am my own city
built on the wrong side
of the tracks,
how I've dreamt of better topography:
seven hills where a woman prays,
a body bathes, young girls dance.

Pixelating at the point of tension
I mottle to slivers of
myself (I don't remember
dying) in

this house.
This house
is nothing like a bird:
no tucking babies under wings
& flying when danger looms,
she is riveted to stone, an architecture of bone.

I cannot swallow an atlas & expect to speak geography.

I want to be anything but
this tired wash of veins
bleeding my chest (a new clutch of
teeth), this child who tastes my
sweet waters (knows not its sinking ships),
the false wintered setting of a cosy diorama.

(I swim right to the horizon where it splits
the world like a razorblade opening a wrist.)

I ask my friends if they too are cities
masquerading as people   if new hearts are
the price for playing empire   if they forget their
own name & bury its sound in their chests.
When baby softens to a comma,
when she, alone again, wonders who she might call,
who she might tell – I'm not okay, yes, again –
she startles, for a moment, remembering the change:
she still knows her girlfriends by their maiden names.

Milk fever

"But you burn, and I know it;
as I throw back my head to take you in
an old transfusion happens again:
divine astronomy is nothing to it."

– ADRIENNE RICH, 'ORION'

the poetry of
ordinary life
set fire to my dreams

I never knew that it could be like this: orbiting each other like painted
polystyrene planets in the neglected hall of the museum; this cast-off string galaxy,
this pockmarked ceiling of parched Prestick & gum,
parquet scarred with polish & earth:
all servants to the sun, who understands the night better than the dark,
plotting a path through the umbaco & cowry constellations.
Orion adored / three sisters abhorred.

Winged night / time crumpling / an old map inking new veins

the pink cave & riotous thirst. I hold the jellied edge of you, translucent, almost imaginary,

small monster; this singing glass / its clean notes & tight breath,

you move & I'm reeled in / serene / curving you around me

like a velvet / your little mouth of night & bone; the mothwing flutter,

lepidopterist's dream / the dreamless sleep pinning me swollen & immobile

queen bee ruling the four corners of her world

Am I a machine a plant an animal ?

a Mean Green Mother from Outer Space?

this photosynthesis becoming me,

it all hurts but I don't know how to say a breeze

is the same as a hurricane   try telling

anyone that being sane rests on a feather

that nothing really is as terrible as the weather

I breathe   my son's name   I bleed knowing
he'll never   hold me   the same
just as I'll only worship true   where new countries
bloom   where our scapulae fit to the coast
& I can fix my mouth to my own breast
& we can hang our names from some other dead tree
believing this will rescue God from pronoun
Heavenly Mother fishboning in my throat
remembering that language is the medium & not the prayer

Nature,
how strident / violent
how unexpected

Thinking   makes it worse   this is the curse
of being   the wick &   not the flame
knowing   the sweetest fruit   of this ancient tree / being unable   to die while so full of life
to return   this is life's sweet paradox: flowers wither after bearing fruit
          to have that living taken
          but they are the fruit too –

don't you see?   there is freedom in the leaving

Translated & multiplied, the poem is not less;
only new, more. In the same world as this,
this world where myth outlives us all,
where we are the dreams of our own writing.
I never wanted to be written alone.
Were we written alone?

You, my child, & me –
like some newly minted coin
circulating a foreign economy –
your mother.

Drinking memory

Growing up, my mother, water diviner
& secret keeper, who looped sunlight through
the sky – who kept old jam jars & fields & fields
of knitting patterns as if one held the template for
happiness – warned me against Ouija boards
& communion with spirits.

We knew that a woman had lingered in the passage
of her childhood home, of a spirit thick as mist
in her bedroom & when I am ten
& playing Glassy-Glassy, my bedroom
takes on the same quality, a cool dense dark;
dusk clotting above my teddy bears & dolls.

In fertile sleep I inherit my mother's dreams,
pleating my nights with the same ribbons of fear
& I am sure that this is no longer my room,
that in 1977 a house climbed into her pocket
& waited its turn to unfold like a letter in a new life
where it thought it could be rewritten.

Catching the sun

You carry your saint beneath your boyfriend's Rip Curl T-shirt;
a silver medallion pressed between breasts padded & pert,

their soft cushion a projection of who you dream you are.
You catch the sun in a mirror, set it roaming far

across cheekbones that in their symmetry are your mother's
only gift, that in their sudden pronouncement carry another

sense: of crop circles & comets. They are painted in brake
fluid you stole from your father's garage, in some late

rite this invocation of spirits, this administration of lith-
ium has sanctioned. The bones, your mother's gift –

– yes, but the Milky Way that you compose on their
alabaster planes is a galaxy all of your own.

Limbic system

water removes
your scent from my skin

but can it remove
the perfect perfume

that clouds
each thought of you?

The last day of Summer

The only words I could muster
when I let you go were

feet are numb.

Not something you're told at the clinic.
Theirs is the provision of four pills, for each
chamber of a mother's bleeding heart; so
in the beginning of the end of us
my only words, in pure shock, in feverish numbness, my cruel epitaph,
(a prayer I chanted while the brufen kicked in

& recorded in the sanctuary of an iPhone note) were:

feet are numb.

I convinced myself that female rabbits will re-absorb their litters,
a last shred of reason (sanity-saving: you do what you've got to do),
circled back into the old familiar pains sharpened with expedience.

And then I released you – into the humid summer night, where you
    returned to the sky,
taking the last of a season's light with you, now distant and eternal as
    the ebb tide.

feet are numb
feet are numb
feet are numb

Nobody's but my own

I sip rooibos my mother has brewed over open flame,
stare out at her garden – wild, indigenous, weeds
pilfering the loving bones of flora known intimately as
her daughters; naked as trees, dancing evangelical – and

walk over to my dressing table built in the sixties for
this auburn-haired girl, my mother all of eleven & more
in love with her father than she ever will be, a man I'll never
meet, but to whom I owe my high forehead & love for violent men.

I stack silver bangles up to both elbows, pause at the mirror
& reach for that lipstick he bought me, in the shade that reminds
me of crushed grapes & sobbing & fucking & danger,
& the time our unborn child circled above our heads.

I open my notebook; savour the slow-ripening
quiet, of a morning that is mine, a small freedom found.

Glass lives (in two parts); or, Don't Anybody Throw Stones, Please

– for my grandmothers

ENSEMBLE

THE PATERNAL GRANDMOTHER: Passed in denial
THE NEIGHBOURS: Present, but say nothing
THE GRANDDAUGHTER: Lives
THE UNWELCOMED: Silver sacs of wine; glass teeth of gin
THE PHOTOGRAPH OVER THE MANTEL: What we know of the
  maternal grandmother

PART I

SCENE I

*At the far end of the plot where we zigzagged after wild rabbits when
the roses curved like tired women and the tangerine linoleum curled to
wood shavings / where the veld lifted like a page worn from thumbing
and the plot tore like a moth eaten map / she sold cold Black Label
quarts to men who would buy and to the others she showed her gun.*

THE GRANDDAUGHTER *[who says all she is permitted to say about
  THE PATERNAL GRANDMOTHER]:*

Your cat eyes   sea green. Cold hands.
        Stable door. Tom cats.
Clutching roses that   bit your hands.

[Afraid to ask how bored she was, prays instead to her like God.]

Marcia,

your name heaves
a cleft in
my tongue: bone-white Vogue
                        between your
                                 lips   like a movie star   (i). Silver screen

bunny ears luring signal   and later you tilt into the bath
a pick splitting ice
your head meets the taps   like neighbours greeting   (ii). Medicine cabinet
a kiss of skull, necking   blood, like Tommy next door
whose radio told him to   kill his wife

[THE PATERNAL GRANDMOTHER says nothing, lifts her glass.]   (iii.) *Clink clink*

THE GRANDDAUGHTER knows THE PHOTOGRAPH OVER THE MANTEL by two names, given and granted. An ungodly weight rests in her bones, bleeds into the younger.

THE GRANDDAUGHTER *[remembering the time her mother cried over an empty vodka bottle in her cupboard]*:

We dip together   in dreams   (iv). Gin / water
in electric dance   halls of grief;
on private stages   of sin, this forgotten
jukebox of   joy.

SCENE III

THE PATERNAL GRANDMOTHER and THE GRANDDAUGHTER have
broken the fast. Ash stains their hairlines. Their skins are cool and
dry as scales. In their fists are potatoes green as earth, glassy with the
promise of sick. They cross themselves in opium, unscrew the papsak
mouth. Locked up, the nuns hiss like snakes. There is a cool rustling.
They empty their bodies of thought. They fill their minds with wine.

THE GRANDDAUGHTER:

(v). Atriums

They say the sunsets on Venus last forever.
They say it's better to live than be buried at all.
They say that a glass of red wine a day keeps the heart attacks at bay.
They say women don't need their own money.
They say that husbands must keep their dear housewives in check.
They say that unlike whiskey, gin has no smell.
They say that tom-cats are the proper bad luck.
They say that nobody can know another's private hell.

THE PATERNAL GRANDMOTHER *[dipping the black, fluted stem into*
   the ashtray as if it were ink]:

They say
They say
They say

ALTOGETHER *[flicking the night across their eyelids. Honey birds*
   settle on their blonde beehives]:

But the rooms in our mouths give it all away.

PART II

SCENE I

There is a boat in a bottle on the mantelpiece.

THE PHOTOGRAPH OVER THE MANTEL *[handing the bottle to her granddaughter, so heavy it takes her two arms to carry although the doors it will unlock are aching to open]*: Sail through the narrow neck and you will find more than our personal histories. Beyond the bottle is a land of gristle and fat, whole worlds I left behind.

THE GRANDDAUGHTER *[seeing the private countries of her family: islands incandescent with grief; deserts smarting with rage]*: Sobriety is so far. And the waters are choppy. The blank-eyed stare of the porthole kisses round wells of stone. We're alone–

[Domed halls of bone and brass loom ahead. In fields of navy cacti, holy fountains are marbled into cool silence. There are courtyards alive as cemeteries, banquet halls sibilant with secrets. Shadows murmur in the stained glass like flies trapped in the web. On a moonstone path a crocodile circles, his belly ticking, a gin bottle knitted to its back. Cupped palms kiss like jealous cousins.]

SCENE II

In the raw tundra of the nearest shore, a cathedral rises like a great glass bird. Around it a fizzing mote circles, sizzling like burning meat.

THE PHOTOGRAPH OVER THE MANTEL *[imagining she could do more than look]*: You can stay with me a little while. With me and the shining ones. I'll teach you all a grandmother can. How our walled gardens are better than none, why you can't fall off the floor.

THE GRANDDAUGHTER *[looking up, alarmed, recognising the phrase, responding]*: And this is why we made intervention our religion. Why we don't believe in strength. Why our priests are broken women. Why our temples have twelve steps. Why we celebrate rock bottom. Why our angels live two weeks. Why our altar has three bar stools. Why it's laid with satin slips. Why our houses have sad faces. Why our bodies are rich with spirits.
And why, and why!

ALTOGETHER *[looking to the stained glass]*: guns and gin are sacrilege.

SCENE III

In a great domed hall, filled with birds, THE GRANDDAUGHTER *and her grandmothers have assembled.*

THE PATERNAL GRANDMOTHER *[her cheeks triangulating against the tip as if she is signing some contract with herself, as if she is rewriting the truth behind the scar above her lip]*:

(vi). Mirrors

Cities contain us
like mothers /
We built these walls so
you can be free.

THE GRANDDAUGHTER *[holding* THE UNWELCOMED, *looking to both her grandmothers]*: And what legacy have you left for your daughters? What song did you sing to soften your tender-heart'd boys? Which song must I sing to keep them that way?

[Nobody responds. There is the sound of static. A woman cries out. Curtains of red velvet flood the stage, blocking it from view.]

New grammar

a medium is simple really   she calls forth   the past
which is metonymy   flesh summoned from the wet skin
of an early spring day   It's simple   *Come, I'll show you*
simple as forgetting what it was
to contain   all the world's longing inside your skin
when you slip so easily
from beloved to   painted blood
a letter   sent away for being itself

Love in the Year of Bleeding

I (*STONE*)

Something is biting me,
a knot mouthing
from inside my blood,
softly crying   *remember,*
resentment brewing in the solar plexus
corrosive as the sun,
mole-blind & urgent,
a radioactive memory
longing for her tongue
to speak silence,
to conjure life when her
fists meet your gums.

II (*KNIFE*)

Do you remember the
first time you bled?
Could you taste colour & did
sound paint a montage on   your eyelids?
I tasted it, your pain, I know
its phosphorescent symmetry,
its colour of love   its feel of home.

Light explodes behind the banana trees,
who like caged birds imitate flight –
their beaks like
blades / their strange
tongues.

III (*SKIN*)

you can't be blamed for teaching me the first lesson,
but you certainly ploughed it through
lacing your love so near &
close / a skin
you plucked / a
chord you sung /
if it doesn't hurt it's not true

IV (*FEATHER*)

When winter begins I ask if you remember your darkest nights
in silence:
this nightshade,
a star burst,
the split   ting
& echo of
every hurt
birthing rain.

love lives
     behind
your eyes
     the place
colour
     bleeds swim
inside
     that spec
tral haze
     tasting
shores heed
     ing the
flood yet
     water
won't wash
     away
the fault
     lines of
a body
     history
interrupts

V (*SALT*)

Feeding a bird doesn't mean it won't die.

your cousin is sick & you're upset about it / I can see how it eats you
/ while the pasta boils you point to the blue in your eyes / a blue of
oceans mid-winter / warmed & shark-thirsty / metal as blood you say
/ God painted your love for us / behind your eyelids / a shutter of
pins / a bed of stone / a belly of rice / the knife rusted to the root /
there are no more stories / I tell you I'm spent / you'll have to feed
yourself now / my blood is done / we forget the strangers of Ko
Tao / & the blood of Ton Sai / & the two tests that sang magenta

that sang our future in a single song that we didn't bother to memorise
tasting the echo of this child in the next
& sealing the test
from the Clicks at Hemingways
in an envelope marked 'Summer'

There are many ways to leave a bruise.
Not all require fists.
Perhaps, a gauge then, is tears.

/

Pain is
knowing sweetness,
& sweetness being
gone.

(I have always known you / even when I didn't)

/

in bed you wrap
    your feeling parts
around me with
    our shadows still
whole as shaded
    gardens
hosting picnics
    bearing bodies
our legs stitching
    together like
roots the light can't
    touch marking the
join with diamonds
    stones immortal
with light

VIII (*ANAMNESIS*)

today I told the doctor you could read my mind / that our dreams
are like rain falling from the same cloud / that our blood has always
longed to flow through the same veins/ & he calls this a symptom
/ accusations fly / a script is written / yet he cannot name what
he doesn't believe / he cannot believe what he'll never know /
that in the flooding there is freedom / in the drying there is life

/

we skim paper lanterns across the satin lagoon
they disperse – confetti, ashes,
all the things we can't say we taste, touch, remember –
in our unnamed life

IX (*FLAME*)

ash won't birth flame anymore
than a cloud will slake thirst

X (*TEMPLE*)

You leave for work. I take our son
to school, your smile rising in his
cake-batter face,
his eyes like bamboo
piercing a quiet lake.
I know genesis has its place –
& wonder if like a bougainvillea,
a city might grow amidst this rubble:
this city a resurrection,
a consecrated kingdom,
this kingdom of rivers,
this river of skin –

in unmarked tombs unsent birthday cards –

& look now at
where we are & look
now at what
our blood has made.

REFERENCES & NOTES

In the poem 'Milk fever,' the line "a Mean Green Mother From Outer Space" is written for a song by the same name that was composed for the film, *The Little Shop of Horrors* (*"I'm just a mean green mother from outer space / Gonna trash your ass! / Gonna rock this place! / I'm mean and green / And I am bad!"*)

The phrase "a haunting we will go" in the poem 'Origin myths' comes from the name of a film featuring Casper the Friendly Ghost, narrated by Frank Gallop and shot by Seymour Kneitel.

'Women with houses for heads' is named for and written as a response to *Femme Maison* (1946-47) a series of drawings and paintings by Louise Bourgeois, in which the heads of naked women have been replaced by architectural structures to depict and explore, among other things, the strictures of domesticity and motherhood on an artist.

'Glass lives...' was inspired by Tennessee Williams' play, *The Glass Menagerie*, with my own Photograph Over the Mantle taking her cue from the one in the play.

Reading Kaveh Akbar's poem, 'Vines', gave me an idea for the images I wanted to conjure for the first part of 'A premonition of a past we haven't written yet'.

Section H in 'Inventory of Dreams' was written with *Beloved* by Toni Morrison in mind, in particular the character Beloved herself.

The line "something other than metaphor / the word itself" in 'New grammar' is a response to Adrienne Rich's line from 'Diving into the Wreck': "the thing I came for: / the wreck and not the story of the wreck / the thing itself and not the myth".

For the form and language of 'Love, in the Year of Bleeding', I am indebted to Ocean Vuong and his poem, 'On Earth We're Briefly Gorgeous', as well as Danez Smith, for their poem, 'Crown', which both lent me word and form with which to write this poem.

The title of 'Mourning Song' alludes to 'Morning Song' by Sylvia Plath.

ACKNOWLEDGEMENTS

Thank you to the following people for their love, support and patience as this book made its way into the world: my parents, Gillian and Tony Ross, who have always encouraged me to dream (and come back down to earth from time to time); my sister, Sasha Ross, thank you for the same, and for berry seasons and cobra and Creme Soda skrikking us at midnight; my son, Oli, who shows me how big love can be every day; and my partner, Chad-Julian Goodall, for loving me plum-crazy.

For all this and incomparable Sunday lunches, thanks must go to the Goodall, Kingma, and Sumption families, especially Ma, Pops and Aunty Cess. Thank you to my Honourary Aunts, Karuna Harry and Anne Smith, and their families, for being my own. Thanks also to the Tennent, Cromhout, Giese, MacDonald, Ross, and Maclear families and to my cousins, especially my darlings Quinton Maclear and Candyce Troye Ross.

Thank you to the editors who have selected several of these poems for publication prior to this book and the literary organisations that have supported my writing, especially Short Story Day Africa, the National Arts Festival Short Sharp Stories Award, *Brittle Paper*, Iceland Writers Retreat, Writivism, and Time of the Writer.

Thank you also to Eliza Reid and Erica Jacobs-Green, for your endless support, and for Iceland, which helped lead me to this point. Thanks also to Miles Moreland for his generosity and support.

Sawadee ka to my Bangkok family, namely Eve Sinhaseni, Cam Browning, and Michala Laohachaiyot, who assured me in the spirit of mai pen rai that I would be okay. You were right.

Thank you to every one of my friends, especially the following, who were around while I gave birth to this book (and a baby):

Calli Roberts, Charmante Pearce, Lauren Footman, Josephine Higgins, Shameez Joubert, Karen Tennent, Amy Moss, Gabriela Cromhout, Chantelle Kean, Lisa Bell, Michal Blaszczyk, Cebokazi Marala, Claire Martin, Megan Dominion (who knew first), Carla Kirk, Geraldine Kent, Francis Brodie, and Laia Frigola Muxach. Not forgetting my hermana, Fidelina Sandoval. To you, Thomas Hellman and your girls (and the third baby, el tercer nino o la tercera nina), I say muchas gracias.

For love and gin and honesty, midnight tea, motherhood and 4 a.m. L trains back to Brooklyn, my coven of writing sisters: Sibongile Fisher, Rachel Zadok and, of course, Efemia Chela.

To my teachers, lecturers, editors, and publishers, Helen Moffett, Brian Garman, Colleen Higgs, Joanne Hichens – thank you for your support, understanding, mentorship, and friendship. Thank you also to my primary and high school English teachers, Di Grimmer and Christalla Ferreira, and especially to Cara Theart, who told me I would write.

And of course to my publisher, editor and friend, Nick Mulgrew, who believed in me and these poems. Your support is everything.

INDEX; OR,

Inventory of dreams

A. Flying over the ocean
white wings shoot out your back / a boy beside you & he too is a bird
he too is a master of skies & even the clouds rejoice / even your mouth is an
embrace & on your lips is the salt the lone sea leaves

/

B. Prophesy
wide-angle shot to shock: in a bath a girl (who looks like me)
is wet to the chest & splitting open her face with a butcher's
knife she pries apart her soft skull peels away the wet skin
travels inside & snuffs out the ventriloquist mouth with her damp hands
& now a cat emerges from her work &–

/

C&D. Teeth & tidal wave
my lips shake
horizon on fire.
teeth tumble out*
this graveyard of gum
tongue   / bathed in splinters
the water has always
been the end   *the end* a
childhood favourite

/

E. Lullaby
grown in the shadows of our mother's longing
ripening under moons too sad to cast light
fruit only comes (from death) after bloom

(Have you noticed how) everything has the faintest smell of vomit (?)

/

F. Flashback
he looked at me like I was fruit that had grown ripe
under his gaze a shining pink pear softening into
tender consumption
& still he stared at me as if he himself
had planted the tree that bore my sweet

/

G. Lucid
I slide a knife
                between my collar bone
                                        & breast
& slice
                                    clean the flesh

I wake lusting for blade.
How freeing, to lose the parts that men love.

/

H. Mediumship
babies in their first form / the spirit bodies / arrive like characters
   invading a novel
they march right in / all expectant,
saying: write me

/

I. Hallucination
bed sheets   / salt on your lips when the sea leaves, gunpowder's sweet kiss
bikini line   / milk thawed & warmed & set out in a bowl for the cat
                         set round in the thick of your
sun-heated breast
vein-blue   / latch
God

/

J. Daydream while baby sleeps
In a field, picking colour. Yellow, its sweet. Yellow our smiles, our joy; shade
of honey spread thick on my lover's arms, his mouth of butter, melting &
quiet, yes, yellow, you are smile's facsimile. We find you in the birthing day,
in the skin of the leaves who wet themselves in first light, the meat of the sun
only just losing its yolk, only now the same as bananas ripe with green only
at the ends. Settling in the hollow of my elbows, wan & thin / a sliver / mango
wetting my lips, & my skin breathes you in coconut, breathes you in milk.

/

K. Nightmare on withdrawal
a maze of coffee rings
& magazines
& I hold a cool blade
to the plump flesh
above my elbow
I press into my skin
& wait   an exquisite pause
before   the first streak of red
& I cut   hacking & hacking

my neighbour looks on
neither of us says a word

/

K. Under general anaesthetic
rows of babies heads wrong neck
of the woods boiled tomatoes skin
four eyes metal mouth choking

/

L. Nightmare during withdrawal
I stand in third person   cruel arabesque
become conjugated   watching the lightly-tanned
arm fall to the floor   stump in the
wilderness of   living room carpet
some feral cat   afraid of all this order
I look at it vagabond   as some foster child
once tended   one final excommunication

/

M. Recurring
the one in New York City although you've not yet been the one where
you're walking head tilted to the skyscrapers hope set at right angles to
your life in this dream every building is the answer to the question you
have asked the world is alight & you are magical & there is nothing
that could take away this feeling of belonging this feeling of home
in every sparkling window & there is nothing that you couldn't be

/

N. Initiation: Rite of passage
I am a hand folding receiving blankets
& cutting sandwiches isosceles
but I soon forget

/

O. Falling
I have been falling in my sleep for as long as I can remember.
In my dream I do not know I am dead or as good as.

~~will not suffice in explaining everything, and nothing will, of course, only to say,~~
~~on the matter of states & variants, that it is only ever a question of survival. By~~
~~this I mean the~~ self-portrait serves as a necessary vanity. ~~If we are to paint it as a~~
~~dreamscape, then so be it, a problematic study may be excused for what it reveals.~~
~~If in this dream, so common, losing teeth, scrambling for the awful splinters, for~~
~~the milk-coloured residue, for the egg-shell variants of incisor in gum, stained by~~
~~antibiotics, chipped by a Brutal Fruit strawpedo eight years prior, which becomes~~
~~so quickly the recurring dream, of the tidal wave, of stepping out into the broad~~
~~green of an~~ ordinary garden, ~~brokered by light and sweet birds who knew better~~
~~than to try leave, who like you, stand on the grass, holding your father's hand, as~~
~~time distils, becoming this one moment, a frozen hour, a minute, who knows, the~~
~~wave never breaks, it is only frozen in arc, and you view it as you might a dome~~
~~placed over a snow-globe, if underneath, noting its terrible shine, the lethal weight,~~
~~hearing the greenery drop to a murmur, knowing this to be the only true thing~~
~~that has ever happened that you can remember:~~ the end ~~but also, the source of a~~
~~stream that sews itself into the lining of your life, a seam in your body that comes~~
~~alive when you need reminding that this = this hour, is a scene you must paint later.~~

One is useless without the other: the minutiae & the romance are a complement. It is
either a broken mouth or a flattened shore & an astrologer will tell you that there is
nothing in the stars about any of it. & if you are clever enough to know, then like every
young girl shocked to find herself in a woman's body you'll guess that there's some note in
there that rings of loss & that trying to find yourself in time will only ever result in more.

POETRY FOR THE PEOPLE

— AVAILABLE NOW —

Liminal by Douglas Reid Skinner

Collective Amnesia by Koleka Putuma

Thungachi by Francine Simon

Modern Rasputin by Rosa Lyster

Prunings by Helen Moffett
CO-WINNER OF THE 2017 SOUTH AFRICAN
LITERARY AWARD FOR POETRY

Questions for the Sea by Stephen Symons
HONOURABLE MENTION FOR THE
2017 GLENNA LUSCHEI PRIZE FOR AFRICAN POETRY

Failing Maths and My Other Crimes by Thabo Jijana
WINNER OF THE 2016 INGRID JONKER PRIZE FOR POETRY

Matric Rage by Genna Gardini
COMMENDED FOR THE 2016 INGRID JONKER PRIZE FOR POETRY

the myth of this is that we're all in this together by Nick Mulgrew

— NEW COLLECTIONS UPCOMING FROM —

PR Anderson, Saleeha Idrees Bamjee, & Siphokazi Jonas

AVAILABLE FROM GOOD BOOKSTORES IN SOUTH AFRICA
& FROM THE AFRICAN BOOKS COLLECTIVE ELSEWHERE

UHLANGAPRESS.CO.ZA

Printed in the United States
By Bookmasters